ELLE GREY STORIES

You have an Elle Grey Story,
right here in your hand!
Surprisingly, when each story was written,
that's not where they were meant to land!

As each word was put down on paper,
they were not written to be edited,
published or shared.
They were simply words from the heart of a mom,
to show her daughter how much she cared...

because what we learn as
children, shapes us as adults...

FROM MY HEART~TO YOUR HANDS...

These stories were written for my daughter, as you may already know,
as a way to help guide and protect her as she grows.

But once they were written, it was decided it was best to share,
so other parents had a way to show *their* children just how much *they* care.

So, here is an Elle Grey Story, written and shared with you.
I truly hope it helps you guide and protect your children, too!

And that it starts important conversations, which otherwise might not have taken place,
and initiates many reasons to share a warm embrace.

I hope that each story gives your child reasons to explore,
and understand their world a little better every time they walk out the door.

And someday they'll be grown, as will my little one,
our time to teach them will be over, that time with them will be done!

These days will go so fast, we must make each one count,
as none of us know how much time we have... None of us know the amount.

These stories were written with that very thought in mind...
That's why they feel different; that's how they were designed!

Some stories are meant to be funny, so your little one might laugh.
They're each filled with some great characters-
My personal favorites are the purple bird and the sweet giraffe!

But you'll see it and feel it, the story at heart...
The loved poured into each one, right from the start!

So enjoy, and please spread the word...
If these stories help you, please make yourself heard!
This way, other parents, grandparents, aunts and uncles too...
Can show the children in their lives how much they love them, just like you got to do!

Again, I hope you enjoy this story and don't forget there are many more.
Use each one to help your children down their path of life...
After all, this is exactly what the Elle Grey Stories are for!

- Elle Grey

because what we learn as children, shapes us as adults...

WORDS

"Sticks and stones can break my bones, but words can break my spirit!"
This is how that old saying should actually read!

Words can be so damaging, more than we can possibly imagine.
But the words we use also have the power to bring so much joy and happiness to others.
When we speak to other people,
we must do our best to always make a choice to be kind,
and we always have a choice, even during those times we are upset. But this rule applies
to ourselves, as well... We must be mindful to the way we treat and talk to ourselves.
Be your own best friend and be kind to yourself!

OUR FRIENDS IN WORDS

Fluffers the Rabbit

Patty the Panda
Lovingly Named By:
Amy K. Takagaki
and Jordan Gonzales

Roary the Lion
Lovingly Named By:
Arya Jakubowski, Julie Andreu
and Kayla Walsh

Patty and Roary were both given their names by our, "Elle Grey Stories World Readers".

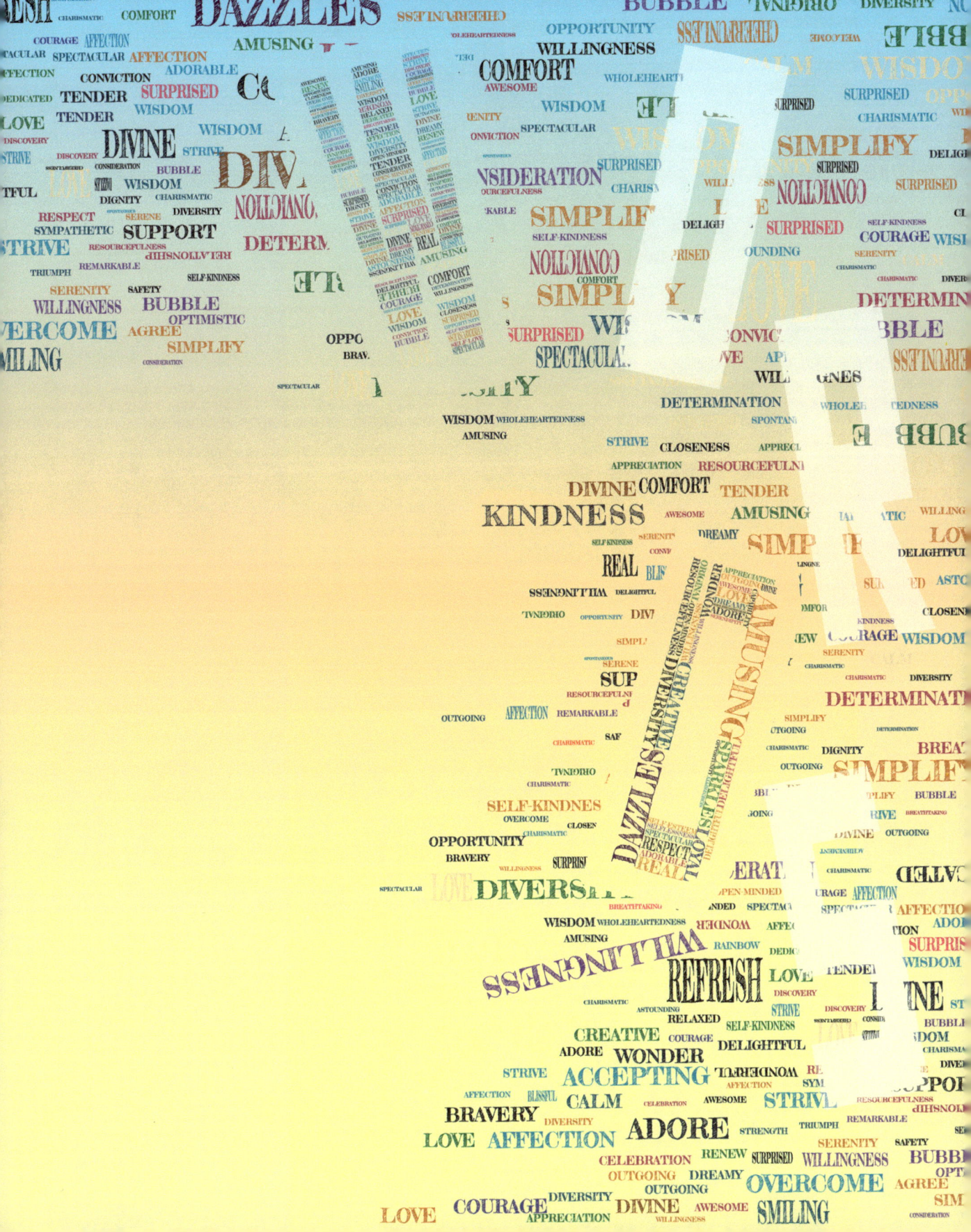

Words

Choose carefully the words that you say,

for those very words may be said to you someday.

Some words are nice,
and others have teeth...

And when you use those,
you can cause others grief.

"These are MINE!
You can't play with them,
you should just leave!"

It's never nice to say words to hurt someone else.

And if you do, you may someday hear those words being said to yourself.

You see, when you are mean to others, that's what can come back to you,

and then others may be mean,
leaving you feeling blue.

It may not happen that day,
it may even take years...

But someday you may hear those same words said to you, and they can leave you in tears.

"These are MINE! You can't play with them, you should just leave!"

So from here on, remember
it's always better to be kind,
and that you always have a choice...
So choose to be nice,
and use your nice voice.

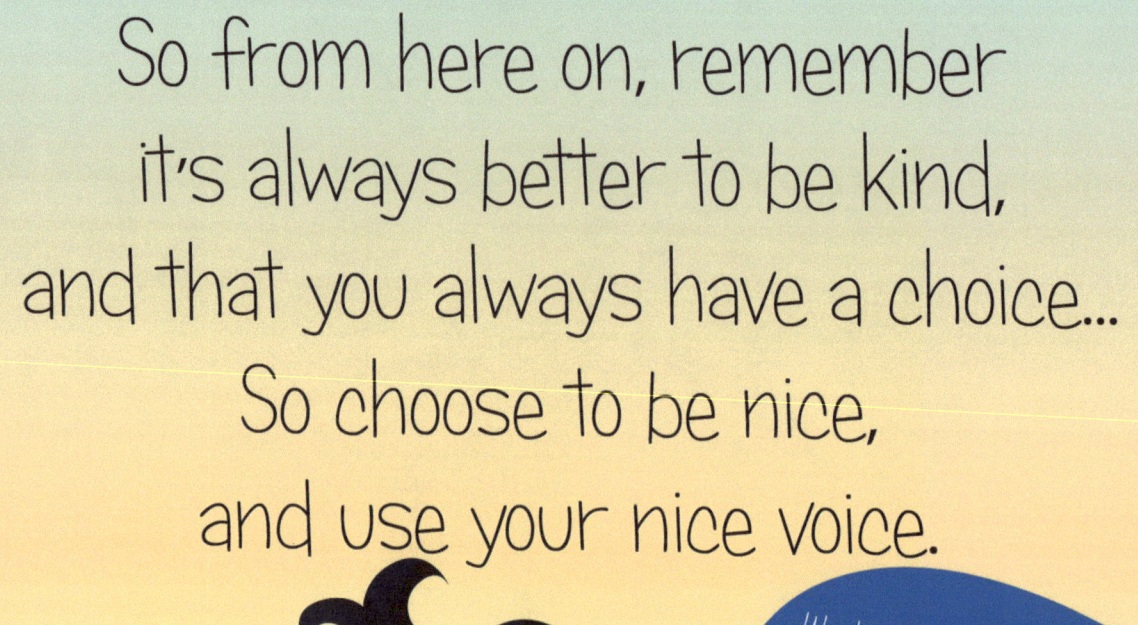

Would you like to play with me? I have lots of toys that we can play with together.

Use words that are gentle—words that are polite.
Do your best to let your voice sound of sweetness and light.

And when that day comes that
you get upset,
keep gentleness in mind...

Just take a moment— take a breath— and then choose to be kind!

LET'S TALK...

Do you think Fluffers the Rabbit was right to forgive Patty the Panda? Why?

Has anyone said mean words to you recently? Tell me all about it.... What happened?

Tell me about a time you said something that wasn't very nice recently. How could you have said or handled it differently?

Tell me about a time recently that you were kind, even when you were upset.

MEET PEANUT, GIGI AND MIA

Characters were created and inspired by the author's daughter, her mother and the author, herself.

Peanut was inspired by Avelle, Elle Grey's daughter. When Avelle was first born, she was so small and her tiny arms and legs took so long to "unfurl", that she resembled a newly hatched baby bird. Peanut is purple like the paint from Avelle's nursery. Her name is Peanut, because when Elle was pregnant, the family referred to her round belly as, "Peanut."

Gigi was inspired by Elle's mother, Avelle's grandmother. She was created in the form of a giraffe because Elle's mother loves giraffes. She is named Gigi because that is the name Avelle gave her, rather than the more traditional, "Grandma".

Mia was inspired by Elle Grey herself. Because she was the creator of the stories, she felt it was symbolic for her to be holding the book. Her name was decided upon as Mia because it was meant to be an acronym for **M**y **I**nspiration, **A**velle. Each of the Elle Grey Stories were originally written as a way to help Avelle through life's challenges, and to instill the values and qualities of the young woman Elle Grey envisioned her daughter becoming one day.

Every story has a surprise ending. This story has one too!

One more kindhearted thought, written just for you!

Always try your very best to be kind.

And not *just* to others...
But also, to your own heart and mind!

NOTE FROM THE AUTHOR

If you feel a story is missing... Perhaps your little one is facing a challenge and there is currently nothing in the Elle Grey Stories Collection to help them- let me know! Just go to www.ElleGreyStories.com/contactus, or visit our Facebook page and write me. I really want to know about it.
Perhaps a new story will be in order for your little one!
Hugs,

Be sure to visit www.ElleGreyStories.com for other titles and collections. You can also learn about Elle Grey and why she wrote the Elle Grey Stories.

I JUST WANT TO THANK ALL OF MY FAMILY FOR THEIR UNWAVERING SUPPORT!

Ken H.
My amazing life partner, an outstanding and loving father to our children
and the man that is always encouraging me to think bigger.
Thank you for believing in me and loving me through it all!

Thomas H.
My wonderful son- full of love, hope, laughs and all around wonderful!

Anthony B.
My wonderful son-he inspires me, keeps my on my toes and always in stitches.

Avelle H.
My darling little girl full of so much life and so much love.
She is the inspiration behind every Elle Grey Story.

Joyce G.
My brave mom... the woman that instilled in me the belief that life is short,
which has allowed me to appreciate every day.
Thank you for always being there with kind words of encouragement!

MY ELLE GREY STORIES BOOK TEAM:

Thank you for all the extra hours and passion you all have poured into this project of love!

Nastasia D.
Nastasia is our lovely Illustrator. She helps bring colorful life to each story.

Anthony B.
Ant is my youngest son and always jumps in to help
with just about everything on the project.

Joyce G.
Joyce is my mom...She pours lots of love into each fluffy friend featured in the stories.

Kimmie M.
Kimmie allows me time to create and makes sure
I get a little sleep after late nights with a little one.

Alison B.
Alison, our editor...she encourages me to be a better writer and always makes me laugh.

Brittany M.
Brittany, our social media guru... she helps to spread our message of love all over the world.

Emio T.
Emio, our Creative Production Director...Through his lens and creativity, comes magic!

Laure W., The Glow Girls, Pedro M., Isabelle B. and Nick B.
My extended team helping me breath real life into Elle Grey Stories!

And a very special thank you to all of you that make up the community
of supporters that believed in the power of these stories
and supported us from the start!

Copyright © 2016 by Elle Grey

All rights reserved. No part of this publication may be reproduced, distributed, or transmitted in any form or by any means, including photocopying, recording, or other electronic or mechanical methods, without the prior written permission of the publisher, except in the case of brief quotations embodied in critical reviews and certain other noncommercial uses permitted by copyright law. For permission requests, write to the publisher, addressed "Attention: Permissions Coordinator" at the address below.

11Eleven Consulting, LLC
11700 West Charleston Boulevard
Suite 170-519
Las Vegas, NV 89135
www.ellegreystories.com

Ordering Information:
Quantity sales. Special discounts are available on quantity purchases by corporations, associations, and others. For details, contact the publisher at the address above. Orders by U.S. trade bookstores and wholesalers. Please contact 11Eleven Consulting or visit www.ellegreystories.com.

Printed in the United States of America

www.ingramcontent.com/pod-product-compliance
Lightning Source LLC
Chambersburg PA
CBHW041503220426
43661CB00016B/1241